200 Words to Help You Talk about Philosophy

Laurence King Publishing

200 WORDS

to Help You Talk about

PHILOSOPHY

Anja Steinbauer

Contents

All or Nothing

Knowledge & Ignorance

Self & Identity

Thought & Language

Good & Bad

Meaning & Purpose

Individuals & Society

Art & Beauty

History of Ideas

All or Nothing

Philosophy

Philosophy is like a washing machine. It takes what is familiar and turns it round and round, leaving it on its head or in a new arrangement, so that you can see it from a different perspective. Philosophy is like dust. It is everywhere and covers everything. There is nothing that is out of bounds for philosophy. We can philosophize about anything from the most banal experiences, such as feeding your dog, to the lofty exploits of science and art. Philosophy is like a fortune cookie: 'Wonder is the feeling of the philosopher, and philosophy begins in wonder,' says Plato. Philosophers are naturally curious and want to find out what is at the heart of things.

Philosopher

In Plato's 'Allegory of the Cave', a group of people live chained up deep inside a cave so that all they can see are shadows on the wall. One breaks free and moves up the cave, gradually realizing how a combination of a fire and objects cast the shadows. Finally, he experiences the sunlit world outside. Excited by his discovery of a truth of which his friends in the cave are ignorant, he returns to them to share his insights. Instead of welcoming him and his message, however, they angrily threaten to kill him. Friedrich Nietzsche knew why: 'The philosopher is a dangerous explosive, in the presence of which nothing is safe.' Philosophy challenges us to examine all our beliefs critically, even the ones by which we have always lived.

Philosophical Problem

How do you make an apple pie? What is an electron microscope? Where is Aruba? If you can look it up in a book or online and get a straightforward answer, chances are it is not a philosophical problem. Philosophical problems tend to lead to further questions. That is both frustrating and useful. By asking questions about questions, we can home in on what exactly the problem is, make it more specific and define its scope and significance. We also come to conclusions in philosophy, but it is very important that these conclusions are subject to further questioning and critical analysis by oneself or others.

Being

What is a glass? You may answer, 'It is a receptacle out of which I drink.' Most of the time you probably don't even notice its existence, and you certainly don't have to think about it. You just use it. However, when it breaks and the milk spills all over your kitchen floor, you will definitely notice it. This, says Martin Heidegger, is when the being of the glass reveals itself to you. Heidegger shows that our primary way of directly engaging with being is practical, not theoretical. The most important answer about the being of the glass comes from thinking about what the glass does for us.

Nothing

Can you think about 'nothing'? Parmenides believed it to be impossible, since as soon as we think about 'nothing' we automatically presuppose 'something': 'You neither understand nor articulate non-being.' And yet, nothing is sometimes a real problem. On one occasion I wanted to take my little son to the circus. We were looking forward to the spectacular sight of the big tent and the colourful hustle and bustle, but when we arrived at the field, the circus had already left. Its non-being was incredibly obvious and important to us. The Daoist philosopher Zhuangzi highlights this importance with a much more practical example: 'Cut doors and windows from the walls of a house; but the ultimate use of the house will depend on that part where nothing exists.'

Metaphysics

Why is there something rather than nothing? What is the nature of reality? Is time real? These are some of the questions metaphysics is about. Arthur Schopenhauer believed that humans are 'metaphysical animals', so we ask these questions as a matter of course. As a discipline within philosophy, metaphysics enquires into the fabric of reality. This means that, for example, the metaphysics of the fictional Star Wars universe would be centrally concerned with the Force, which, as we all know, 'holds the galaxy together'.

World

Sometimes, it looks as though philosophers are just stating the obvious. Ludwig Wittgenstein begins a celebrated book with the famous statement: 'The world is all that is the case.' He points out that we shouldn't think of the world as a collection of things, but as being composed of relational arrangements, 'states of affairs'. There are many other fundamental questions to be asked, such as whether the world is fundamentally a static structure where change is insignificant – since, whatever happens, the world is always the world – or a constantly changing entity.

Cosmos

Are you a tidy person? Well-organized? Efficient? Even if you aren't, chances are that you value a certain amount of order, simply because it makes life easier. Ida keeps her socks in a chaotic jumble in a drawer. Cyrus's sock drawer, by contrast, keeps like with like, pairs together, grouping wintry warm socks, formal dark socks, tennis socks, all in their place. It's easy to see what's what. The idea of a 'cosmos' assumes that the world is like Cyrus's sock collection, rather than Ida's. In a way, it makes philosophy possible; it implies that the world is not random but a structured and organized whole that can be understood by human intellect.

Mind

We often think of the mind as something other than and superior to the body, as in 'mind over matter'. Surely, thinking and having ideas must be different in nature from riding a bicycle or eating a cream cake? Gilbert Ryle thought this was a mistake, a 'philosopher's myth'. He went so far as to describe the idea of a non-physical mind with a great metaphor – the 'ghost in the machine'. Ryle believed that all human functioning can be described as 'acts' and that there is no division between mental and physical acts. So mental processes are just intelligent acts. Could we even say that the mind is just the brain?

Dao (Tao)

'What is the Dao?' is the central question of classical Chinese philosophy. Traditional Chinese philosophy does not assume, as much of Western philosophy does, that the world can be understood as a complex static structure; instead, reality is seen as change, movement, transformation, being in constant flux. It is a process. This process is called the Dao (or Tao). The term can also be applied to the natural course of aspects of reality, such as 'the Dao of human beings' or 'the Dao of the father'. These examples suggest that there is a 'natural' way to be human or to be a father.

Samsara

The idea of *samsara*, 'wandering,' is an underlying assumption in a number of Indian belief systems, and forms the basis of the Buddhist world view. It reflects the thought that a constant cycle of rebirth keeps us chained to this world of impermanence and suffering. The Buddha's four noble truths reveal that this is not a necessary process, but that the cycle can be broken. The so-called eightfold path suggests a combination of life choices based on wisdom, ethics and meditation to effect this change. This, as well as the related idea of 'karma', suggests that the universe has moral elements. In other words, what I do will affect the world.

Chaos

In our ordinary use of the word, 'chaos' gets a very bad press. We tend to think of it as the absence of order, a total and irredeemable mess. However, it can be a good thing. It is a state of disorder with seemingly unlimited potential. 'Chaos', according to Hesiod, denotes a yawning abyss, the beginning of the world, both frightening and full of promise. Aristotle thought of it as unformed matter, that from which all things are ultimately formed – creative chaos.

Consciousness

Since you are reading this right now, there is no doubt that you are conscious. Being conscious is not hard to do, but it is hard to describe. Consciousness is an umbrella term that covers a variety of mental acts, including thought, memory and imagination. There are a number of difficulties that philosophers try to figure out. Thomas Henry Huxley observes: 'How it is that anything so remarkable as a state of consciousness comes about as a result of irritating nervous tissue, is just as unaccountable as the appearance of the Djin, when Aladdin rubbed his lamp.'

Zombies

Zombies are known to be brain-eating, undead monsters, unfashionably dressed and stumbling around uncontrollably. However, David Chalmers assures us that 'philosophical zombies' are not the same as 'Hollywood zombies'. Philosophical zombies seem just like everybody else, with one big difference: they lack consciousness. While they can act and interact in the same way as other people, they have no inner awareness or understanding of what it is they do. A number of philosophical points can be made using the zombie thought experiment. For example, if zombies really are logically conceivable, the mind cannot just be the brain. Furthermore, they illustrate the problem of 'other minds': how can I know that you are not a zombie?

Intentionality

How do you know you're conscious right now? It is because you're reading this book. Maybe you're also aware of your chair being slightly uncomfortable, of the sound of traffic in the distance, of being thirsty. We're never simply conscious, we're always conscious *of* something. In other words, all forms of conscious experience are 'intentional', and consciousness is always directed at objects. Franz Brentano believed intentionality to be the defining feature of the human mind, 'the mark of the mental'.

Time

Lars has been waiting for half an hour. He's checking the time again; it seems more like an hour to him. Why is Finn not here yet? Augustine tells us that time is mainly memory and the future is expectation, so both are dependent on a human mind. John McTaggart builds on this by imagining two parallel time lines or 'series'. The first is subjective, running from the past over the present to the future: Lars remembers arranging to meet Finn, he is now waiting and he intends to tell Finn off when he arrives. McTaggart's second time line is objective and consists of events that happen before, simultaneously with or after another event. Once they have happened, the sequence is forever fixed. McTaggart thought that time could not be explained by just one of the two series, and both were 'essential to the reality of time'.

Change

Heraclitus gives articulate expression to the experience of change: 'On those stepping into rivers staying the same other and other waters flow.' The tantalizing paradox here is that the river both does and does not change. What is the reality of change, and how deep does it reach? For Aristotle, time is the key to understanding change. It is tied to motion. When we think about change, we tend to think about motion over time, such as the hands of a clock moving or a flower growing, blooming and withering.

Causation

How does one event cause another? David Hume suggested that perhaps causality is only observed regularity, such as one billiard ball moving when struck by another. The problem is to distinguish between regular events that are causally connected and others that are not. For example, every morning my alarm clock rings at 6am and I wake up. But before my alarm goes off, Gill in Leicester leaves her house to go jogging. Although my waking up is an effect of the alarm clock ringing, Gill is not a cause of the alarm clock. David Lewis might have a solution. His counterfactual theory says that an event causally depends on another only if it would not occur without it.

History

'Philosophy is its time grasped in thought,' the philosopher G.W.F. Hegel claims. 'History is philosophy teaching by examples,' the historian Thucydides explains. If one or both of them are right, there is a strong connection between philosophy and history. The philosopher tells us that philosophy is essentially historical and the historian that history is decidedly philosophical. Giambattista Vico believed that history followed the same cycle over and over again: 'Men feel necessity, then look for utility, next attend to comfort, still later amuse themselves with pleasure, thence grow dissolute in luxury, and finally go mad and waste their substance.' Is there ever anything new?

Idealism

Are ideas as real as a chair or table? Idealists argue that not only are they as real, in fact they are more real. Although there are different kinds of idealist, they all hold that reality is mind-dependent. For example, George Berkeley claimed that 'to be is to be perceived'. In his view, the chair is real *because* I observe it. What he means is this: imagine a chair you couldn't see or sit on, you couldn't touch or otherwise perceive. You might as well say, 'There is no chair.' That is why Berkeley says that our perception is what being is all about. What you cannot perceive does not exist.

Physicalism

Do you think everything in the world is subject to the laws of physics? If so, you are a physicalist. On the whole, physicalists subscribe to a naturalist view of the world, saying that all things and events in the world can be, or will ultimately be, explained by science. This is uncontroversial when we think about magnetic forces, bugs or diseases. However, what about dreams, love, poetry or religion? Do the laws of science apply to these areas of our lives, or are they independent of them?

Dualism

You cannot touch thoughts or smell memories. Isn't it intuitive to conclude that there are two different kinds of thing in the world, 'mind' things and 'body' things? Dualism is a way of describing reality. It comes in different varieties, but substance dualism, its strongest form, implies that there are two kinds of thing – physical things, such as tables, and non-physical things, such as souls – which are totally separate from each other. If that is so, dualists must explain to us how they can interact. After all, a physical headache will interfere with my thoughts, and my thoughts can control my body. How is that possible?

Eternity

While we often think of eternity as endless duration, such as in 'an eternity of boredom', in philosophy it is used in a different sense. Here, it means 'outside time and space'. In the past, philosophers have often assumed that there is an eternal realm, contrasting with our world of constant change. This could be the realm of a divine being or of reason or even of mathematical objects.

Infinity

The early Greek thinker Zeno of Elea presented philosophers for generations to come with a bombshell by introducing a number of mind-boggling paradoxes concerning change and motion. For example, he suggests that in a race between Achilles and a tortoise, if we assume that Achilles would graciously give the tortoise a small head start, the famous hero would never be able to catch up with the leisurely reptile. Zeno explained this by pointing out that Achilles has an infinite number of places to reach before he can draw level with the tortoise. Since then, even more controversial ideas of infinity have emerged, from the infinite density of black holes to the infinite and uncountable set of real numbers. How many coherent ideas of infinity might we find?

Possible Worlds

Dr Pangloss, a fictional character in Voltaire's satirical novella *Candide*, keeps reassuring everybody around him that, despite numerous calamities that befall them, they all live in 'the best of all possible worlds'. Pangloss is a thinly veiled parody of Voltaire's fellow Enlightenment philosopher Gottfried Leibniz, who made a rational argument in favour of our world, although not perfect, having to be the best that could have been created. In recent philosophy, the idea of possible worlds is used in modal logic to explore metaphysical possibility. Saul Kripke says that 'modal facts' are facts *about* possible worlds, where our actual world is only one among many worlds that are possible. Each possible world is described by a consistent set of statements. So, the statement 'It is possible for me to become a prima ballerina' is true because there is at least one possible world, so defined, where I am a prima ballerina.

Knowledge & Ignorance

Epistemology

Faust, the celebrated scholar of German legend, dedicated his life to the pursuit of knowledge and achieved mastery of all the sciences of his time. But it was all for nothing, he realizes. He is in despair, because he believes that we cannot know anything worthwhile. Can philosophy help? Epistemology is also called the Theory of Knowledge. Here we ask: what can we know? How can we know it? Can we really know anything at all? Isn't Einstein right when he warns us that 'whoever undertakes to set himself up as a judge of Truth and Knowledge is shipwrecked by the laughter of the gods'?

Knowledge

Can knowledge be defined? What does it take to know something? The traditional Western definition of knowledge, with its roots in Plato's thinking, is 'justified, true belief'. In other words, you only really know something if you have good reasons for believing it and, if it is true, you cannot know a falsehood. So, what do you know? I know that the sky is blue, that Christmas is on 25 December, that my dog will bark when the doorbell rings. Each of these claims relies on different kinds of justification, and the question about appropriate justification itself can throw a serious spanner in the works of knowledge claims. Edmund Gettier points out that sometimes beliefs that are justified and true are still not knowledge. For example,

I may believe that it is 10 o'clock, because that is what my kitchen clock shows. However, unbeknown to me, the clock stopped yesterday at the same time. So, while it may be true that it is 10 o'clock, and while I am justified in my belief, I do not actually know it.

Learning

How you learn depends on a number of things, including what kind of learner you are and what kind of thing you're trying to learn. Some things, Zhuangzi believed, cannot be learned in a traditional way but must be spontaneously experienced. He tells us about a wheelwright called Bian who explains that, although he can teach his son techniques for fashioning a perfectly round wheel, there is a knack in doing so successfully that cannot be communicated but can be acquired only by doing. He criticizes his scholar–ruler for trying to learn the wisdom of the ancients from books, arguing that what is truly vital to their message cannot be found in their words.

Objectivity

Karl Popper tries to make sense of the idea of objective knowledge by means of the following model. He imagines that our lives take place in three realms or 'worlds': the world of physical objects; the world of subjective knowledge, thought and emotion; and the world of objective knowledge, which is the world of culture and shared ideas. For example, by observation and experimentation in the physical world, a scientist might formulate a theory in the subjective realm and subsequently publish it, releasing it into the world of objective knowledge, where it will be discussed and may eventually have a real-life impact on the physical world.

Subjectivity

'What is it like to be a bat?', asks Thomas Nagel. He is challenging us to acknowledge the special nature of subjective experience. While reductionists believe that everything can be reduced to the language of science, Nagel disagrees. He argues that 'an organism has conscious mental states if and only if there is something that it is like to *be* that organism – something it is like *for* the organism', and, he believes, this cannot be known by external observation. So, even if you were to study my brain while I was drinking a cup of coffee, you could not find out what drinking coffee is like *for me*.

Appearance

One of the most fundamental philosophical worries is that the world may not at all be as it presents itself to us. Plato's 'philosophical doubt' makes clear that what is obvious is not necessarily real. We must therefore distinguish between reality and appearance. So, can we know the world as it really is? Immanuel Kant believed that we are forever tied to our own humanity, and that it is only through the filter of our human senses and ways of thinking that we experience the world. He likened it to permanently wearing green goggles. We can't take our human 'goggles' off, and will only ever know what the world is like for humans.

Ignorance

Adam and Eve had a nice existence, there in the Garden of Eden: no work, no strife and, above all, nothing to worry about. There was only truth, but no opinion; only agreement, no disagreement. They were happy. They were innocent. But they were also ignorant. Ignorance is the price you pay for innocence. The fruit from the tree of knowledge changed all this. It made human lives harder and childbirth painful, but it also made philosophy possible. Although philosophy literally means 'love of wisdom', ignorance has an important part to play. There are many different kinds of ignorance, some bad, some surprisingly worthwhile.

Wisdom

The Oracle of Delphi had made an astounding new pronouncement. It concerned Socrates, the barefoot, ugly, annoying philosopher who haunted the Athenian marketplace engaging unsuspecting passers-by in mind-scrambling discussions. This self-declared gadfly of Athens, the Oracle revealed, was in fact the wisest man of his age! Nobody was more surprised than Socrates himself, who immediately embarked on a research project, seeking out all others who had the reputation of being wise. Here is what happened each time: 'I thought to myself: I am wiser than this man; although I do not suppose that either of us knows anything really beautiful and good, I am better off than he is. For he knows nothing, and thinks that he knows. I neither know nor think that I know.'

Reason

Plato introduced into our civilization a model of the human psyche that has shaped our thinking ever since. He says our souls are like chariots drawn by two horses. One of the horses is obedient, the other wild and in constant need of controlling. This is why it is important to have an able and vigilant charioteer in charge. The charioteer is reason, which must be in control of all thoughts and actions, otherwise the wild horse – our desires – will run amok. Other thinkers have denied that reason can straightforwardly be in control. David Hume, for example, tells us that 'reason is, and ought only to be, the slave of the passions'.

Scepticism

Philosophers love scepticism, because it is the discipline of critical questioning. They also love Pyrrho, the original and most extreme sceptic, because he was so respected that the authorities of his time passed a decree by which all philosophers were made immune from taxation. Pyrrho can teach us all about how to be a sceptic. He questioned everything, but never gave up his search for the truth. Since everything can be doubted and knowledge or certainty seems impossible if your standards are as high as they should be, the best we can do is suspend judgement. Pyrrho believed that this absence of beliefs and values led to an absence of emotional turmoil, and therefore to peace of mind.

Doubt

What can you know for certain? Modern sceptics are more selective and systematic in their application of philosophical doubt than their classical counterparts. René Descartes made use of radical scepticism – doubting everything – but only to get out of scepticism; he wanted to find out what we can truly know. In order to do this, he imagined his beliefs to be like a basket of apples. The best method for separating the good ones from the rotten ones is to empty out the whole basket and put only the good ones back.

Error

In his efforts to work out principles for a scientific method, Francis Bacon warns thinkers to beware of the following false notions, which he calls 'idols'. 'Idols of the Tribe' were fallacies in humankind, most notably man's tendency to believe that nature was ordered to a higher degree than it actually was. 'Idols of the Cave' were misconceptions inherent in individuals' thoughts, spawned by private prejudice. 'Idols of the Marketplace' were errors that arose from received systems of thought. 'Idols of the Theatre' were errors spawned by the influence of mere words over the human mind.

Prejudice

While Cicero believed prejudice to be the result of manipulation, Francis Bacon characterized prejudice as a 'false mirror', an error to which we are all susceptible. Voltaire illustrates the contrast between prejudice and good judgement: 'But it is through prejudice that you will respect a man dressed in certain clothes, walking gravely, and talking at the same time. Your parents have told you that you must bend to this man; you respect him before you know whether he merits your respect; you grow in age and knowledge; you perceive that this man is a quack, made up of pride, interest, and artifice; you despise that which you revered, and prejudice yields to judgement.'

Experience

Human experience is diverse; it includes perception, emotion, association and perhaps even the controversial 'religious experiences'. In contrast to rationalist philosophers, who believe that knowledge can sometimes come from reasoning alone, empiricist philosophers believe that all knowledge comes originally from sense experience. John Locke puts it: 'Nothing is in the intellect that was not first in the senses.' Analysis of even the most complex ideas will demonstrate that they are only combinations of sense impressions.

Science

Science is the rational and systematic investigation into aspects of the natural world using measurement and evidence. But how does scientific development happen? Thomas Kuhn believed that science can be described as a process with distinct phases in which scientists will work within the context of shared assumptions – a 'paradigm' – to research and produce predictions. Eventually, this period of 'normal science' comes to a halt and a new paradigm is adopted that will allow scientists to return to 'normal' scientific activity and work productively. Scientists who cling to outdated paradigms will no longer find work. An example would be the replacement of steady-state theory with Big Bang theory.

Scientific Method

Has it ever occurred to you that Einstein and an amoeba might have more in common than meets the eye? Karl Popper argues that they use the same method of gathering data, the trial-and-error method. The big difference is that the amoeba will try randomly, while Einstein will use the method selectively. Popper calls this 'critical rationalism'. Its basis is in everyday life, since Popper believes that 'all life is problem-solving'. Scientists engage in a refined and more stringent form of problem-solving; they form hypotheses and test them by means of observation and experimentation. If a hypothesis fails, they try something else.

Falsification

'The room is full of pink fluffy monsters that only I can see' cannot be a scientific statement. Why not? First of all, it is not testable. It cannot be verified. More importantly, however, it cannot be 'falsified'. Can statements ever be verified? The positivists of the Vienna Circle thought so, but Karl Popper disagreed; even with an abundance of data, he maintained, you can never conclusively prove a theory to be right. What makes it scientific is its potential to be disproven. Here is a standard example. Initial observation of swans may lead us to the hypothesis that 'all swans are white'. The subsequent discovery of black swans falsifies it, so that a better one can replace it: 'All swans are either black or white.'

Self &
Identity

Human Nature

What is meant by 'human nature'? Is it what is innate in all humans, or is it what sets humans apart from other animals? Traditional Chinese philosophy has little interest in the subject, and yet it is there that one of the most interesting discussions concerning human nature is fought out. The Confucian philosopher Mengzi (Mencius) believed human nature to contain the beginnings of morality, and defended this view against his friend and opponent in the debate, Gaozi, who believed that human nature is neither good nor bad. Another Confucian philosopher, Xunzi, later argued that human nature is bad. Since observation of human behaviour can lend evidence to all these options, perhaps we can never settle this question.

Body

Does your body matter to who you think you are? For most of its history, philosophy has not attributed much importance to the body. It is simply part of the physical world, contrasting with the mind, which is traditionally seen as the true seat of the self. Feminist philosophers have paid more attention to the body, since conventional thinking associated women with the body more than men. Physical attributes such as beauty, as well as the capability of giving birth, have been central to how women are perceived. Exploring relationships between corporeality, self-image and identity is a focal interest of feminist thinkers, one that they share with critical race theorists and philosophers exploring gender diversity.

Soul

The soul is a concept that is familiar to us all, yet it is extremely difficult to pin down. Definitions of 'soul' are varied. For example, Plato believed it to be immortal; he thought it entered the body at birth and left it at death, ready eventually to be re-embodied. Aristotle, by contrast, imagined the soul to be a life force that emerged and died together with the body. Many philosophers today are sceptical about the existence of a soul. They ask what we're looking for, when we talk about the soul. Since it is not physical, it is hard to describe what kind of thing it might be.

Personal Identity

Who are you? Are you the same person you were yesterday or 20 years ago? Ancient Greek philosophers give us a great illustration of the problem of personal identity. Imagine the old, now disused, ship of the hero Theseus slowly rotting away, and each ruined plank being substituted with a new one as needed, until all parts of the vessel have been replaced. Is it still the same ship? If not, when in the process did it cease to be the ship of Theseus? The same question can be asked of us. Over the course of our lives, all our physical and mental attributes change. I don't have anything in common with the baby I once was: neither my body, nor my behaviour, nor my emotions or thoughts are even remotely reminiscent of that infant. What allows me to claim that the baby in a photo is 'me'?

Memory

How lucky we are to be able to remember and recall facts, events and other information, since this comes in very handy in our everyday lives. Philosophers have always believed that memory is important to knowledge, but it is very difficult to work out exactly how this connection works. John Locke was convinced that memory has another important function; it is how personal identity is secured. I know that I am the same person who went to bed last night, because I can remember doing so. Moreover, those experiences that I consider *mine* are those that I can remember having.

Gender

While 'sex' is a biological term, 'gender' is a social category. What makes me a 'woman'? Simone de Beauvoir explains: 'A Woman is not born. She is made.' 'Gender' consequently refers to socially constructed roles that we all have to play, which express themselves in behaviour, expectations and qualities that a society deems appropriate for women or men. Even a much earlier thinker, Mary Wollstonecraft, discusses in detail the harm that gender roles do to all individuals, regardless of their sex, and the difficulties in identifying and casting off their influence. For example: 'Taught from infancy that beauty is woman's sceptre, the mind shapes itself to the body, and roaming round its gilt cage, only seeks to adorn its prison.'

Feminism

Philosophical feminism is a vast and diverse field of study. There is plenty of work for feminist philosophers to do; they are opening up new questions and perspectives in all areas of philosophy. Also, most older philosophy was written by men, so feminist philosophers study how ideas of gender have shaped traditional philosophical concepts. For example, when historical philosophers talk about 'human beings', are they not specifically describing men? In some cases, this becomes particularly obvious as philosophers struggle to accommodate women in the category of 'humans'. Other feminist scholars rethink traditional accounts of the history of philosophy, where the contributions of women have been written out of the canon.

Disability

The philosophy of disability challenges us to consider the issues of a good and dignified life for disabled individuals, but in doing so does much more. It challenges us to rethink questions of knowledge, ethics, social arrangements and politics. Anita Silvers says that 'the moral challenge of disability is to reshape practices so they no longer exclude people with corporeal or cognitive anomalies', and that 'it raises difficult threshold questions about the extent to which the classification is based on biology or is socially constructed'. This means that the philosophy of disability has the potential to change philosophy in general.

Character

Is your character fixed? Can you help being you? Or can you make yourself into the kind of person you choose to be? Aristotle, along with many other moral philosophers, believed that humans have the potential to make themselves into what they choose to be. What it requires is self-awareness, good role models and lots of practice. However, can we really ever change? There are many possible objections to Aristotle's optimism. A first point of criticism may be to say that we don't really have enough insight into who we are. Furthermore, what constitutes change in an individual? Will any change we make to our behaviour make a lasting difference to who we are?

Alienation

Sometimes we relate to the world around us, to other people or even to ourselves in a strangely distant way. Alienation is the experience of being unable to relate or connect to something that ought to be familiar. Certain conditions can cause us to feel alienated. Karl Marx believed that unbridled capitalism had such an effect. In a capitalist society we suffer several forms of alienation. If labour is punishing and repetitive, we are alienated both from our productive activity and from the product of our work. Owing to competition and economic hardship, we are alienated from other people. Finally, we are even alienated from our own humanity.

Dignity

What makes a human life valuable? The idea of human dignity tries to make sense of this question. It is a value that attaches to all human life, regardless of individual differences, social status, gender or age. Beings with dignity deserve respect. But all this still doesn't explain where dignity comes from. Immanuel Kant believed it comes from our ability to make free moral decisions. Even if we do not always make good choices, we have the potential to co-create our world and make a positive contribution as moral agents. 'Dignity' is at the root of a number of important ideas that are prominent in our world, such as that of human rights, the rights we possess as a consequence of human dignity.

Freedom

Jean-Paul Sartre declares that we are 'condemned to be free'. He clearly believed this to be not an advantage but a burden. Other philosophers through the ages have made different assessments of the meaning of freedom to human life. But how free are we? In many ways, we are clearly not free, but are bound by physical and biological necessities. I cannot simply decide to fly around the room, nor can I decide never to sleep again. On the other hand, we are free to make decisions in our lives, and many philosophers would argue that this ability to choose is central to our humanity and moral status.

Fatalism

Imagine you are on a skiing holiday. You are standing on top of the mountain and there is a choice of slopes that you can go down. Fatalism is the view that whichever you choose, you will end up at the same point at the bottom. In other words, whatever life choices I make, they won't make a difference to the way my life eventually turns out.

Determinism

Are you enjoying a cup of coffee while reading this?
Or perhaps tea? Perhaps you have decided not to
have any drinks. It might seem to you that your choice
of beverage, toothpaste, hobbies, friends, sexual
partners and so on is yours and yours alone. However,
determinists insist that things are not as they seem.
Determinism, in contrast to fatalism, does not claim
that outcomes will always be the same. Rather, it says
that because you are part of the physical universe, every
action is subject to the laws of nature and therefore
comes about unavoidably owing to a chain of causes and
effects stretching into the distant past. All this, some
say, means you have no free choice at all.

Death

Not everybody will agree with Martin Heidegger that
thinking about death is a good idea. Heidegger thought
that engaging with our mortality would give us a better
perspective on life. However, thinking about our own
death gives many of us the creeps. The Epicurean
philosophers even thought that the unnecessary fear
of death could spoil your life. Lucretius came up with
arguments to help us out and show that death is not
to be feared. He reminds us that while we're alive death
is not there, and once death is there, we won't be. So,
in either case, there is nothing to worry about.

Immortality

Can we live forever? Can we survive our own deaths?
Is the question of immortality meaningful at all? Woody
Allen clarifies what personal survival means: 'I don't
want to achieve immortality through my work; I want
to achieve immortality through not dying. I don't want
to live on in the hearts of my countrymen; I want to live
on in my apartment.' Immanuel Kant is sympathetic
to this sentiment and says that it is only human to be
curious about immortality, but at the same time he
shoots us down by insisting that we cannot think about
it meaningfully. We will just have to wait and see.

Thought
& Language

Thought

Heraclitus, one of the earliest philosophers of the Western tradition, claims that 'thinking is common to all'. The fact that all humans are thinking beings is uncontroversial. But what about artificial intelligence? Will it require us to rethink what it means to think? John Searle's 'Chinese Room' thought experiment explores this. Imagine a locked room containing a person who neither reads nor speaks Chinese. He has a supply of Chinese ideograms, and a rule book in his own language that tells him how to manipulate them. From time to time, messages in Chinese are passed into the room and he uses the equipment to send back answers that look competent to anyone outside the room. However, the man in the room has no idea what the messages say.

Logic

To philosophize means to think well, to use logic. Logic is the method of philosophy. There are many useful rules to follow if we want to avoid mistakes in our thinking. The four main principles of logic are the following: 1. The principle of identity says that each thing is identical with itself. 2. The law of contradiction says it is impossible for both A and not A to be true. 3. The law of the excluded middle states that either A or its contradiction, not A, must be true, there being no possible middle ground. 4. Finally, the principle of sufficient reason tells us that everything must have a reason or cause.

Truth

'Truth' is a quality not of things in the world but of our statements about the world. In other words, the truth is not 'out there', but is integral to our utterances. Objects in the world simply are or are not. What we say about them, however, is either true or false. How do we know if a statement is true? Much philosophical ink has been spilled on this. Statements that do not make any logical sense have little chance of being true. Furthermore, common-sense experience also helps. In a nutshell, a statement is true if reality confirms it; the cat is on the mat if, and only if, the cat is on the mat.

Truth Criterion

To evaluate a claim, we need standards by which to judge its accuracy: truth criteria. There are several competing theories of truth that give us such standards, most importantly the correspondence theory and the coherence theory. The correspondence theory compares our assertions to states of affairs in the world. The coherence theory says a statement is true if it agrees with all the other facts we already believe to be true. If I want to confirm a set of directions to the zoo, correspondence will require me to follow them and see if they really take me there, whereas coherence will oblige me to look at a map or refer to the system of postcodes.

Dialectic

Plato wrote dialogues in which Socrates discusses ideas with individuals who didn't share his philosophical views. Clearly, Plato believed that the best way of doing philosophy was to have a constructive dialogue. He wanted to depart from the practice of thinkers producing long monologues spinning out their theories. How can we have constructive dialogues? This is what the dialectic is about. It means a movement between two extremes or opposing opinions. By listening and responding to each other, both sides can learn. Together, they can progress towards the truth.

Rationality

How rational are we? Do we act in accordance with good reasons? As it turns out, there are numerous ways of being rational. Max Weber defined four different model types of rationality that we use in our social interactions: 1. Instrumental rationality makes use of our informed expectations about the behaviour of other human beings or objects to achieve 'rationally pursued and calculated' ends. 2. Value rationality motivates us to take action on the basis of moral, aesthetic or religious values, independent of the chances of success. 3. Affectual rationality is emotion-led. 4. Conventional rationality prompts us to act according to ingrained patterns and habits.

Irrationality

Philosophers from Plato to René Descartes have assumed that the human psyche contains a non-rational element that either is impervious to reason, and therefore irrational, or can be educated by reason and made rational. But Blaise Pascal argues that there may be rationality *in* irrationality: 'The heart has its reasons which reason cannot know.' Some philosophers, including Zhuangzi and Friedrich Nietzsche, defend the importance of irrationality in our lives, but in surprisingly rational ways.

Analysis

Analysis is an important tool for any thinker. It is the process of systematically exploring a subject in all its facets, carefully preserving its structure and distinguishing between different elements with respect to their importance and explanatory potential. When we analyse arguments, for example, we distinguish carefully between reasons and conclusions, and study how they are connected. When we analyse a situation, likewise we distinguish between salient and accidental features in the light of what we try to explain.

Argument

In philosophy and critical thinking, an argument is not a dispute, a shouting match or a falling-out. In Monty Python's 'Argument Clinic' sketch, one person repeatedly denies anything the other one says. This kind of 'no – yes – no' exchange just won't do for us. In order for you to be arguing, you must do more than simply disagree. You must put forward reasons that say why you disagree and that provide evidence for your point of view.

Conclusion

A conclusion is a belief or decision reached as a result of a reasoning process. The move from reasons to a conclusion is known as an 'inference'. Philosophers spend much time thinking about how reasons and conclusions are connected and when an inference can be legitimately performed. Conclusions do not always come in the form that you might expect. Advertising is a good example. A television advert showing a flashy car driving through a dramatic landscape is not just there to show you a pretty little film. It is an argument, the intended conclusion of which is 'buy this car'.

Reasons

'Reasons' or 'premises' are statements that are given in favour of a conclusion. They must be acceptable and relevant and provide good grounds for the conclusion. The most important thing I will say to you in this whole book has to do with reasons, and it is this: in order to agree or disagree meaningfully with what someone says, you must engage with their reasons, especially if you disagree. It is not enough to say that you don't like their conclusion; in order to show that they are wrong, you must critique their reasons. We have to train ourselves to pay attention to *why* people believe something, rather than just *what* they believe.

Assumption

In critical thinking, 'assumption' is an unspoken reason that the arguer needs for the conclusion to stand. Being aware of unstated assumptions is very important for critical debate. Take this example, which is very familiar in the abortion debate: 'Killing an innocent person is wrong; therefore, abortion is wrong.' The arguer clearly assumes that a foetus is a person, otherwise the conclusion could not work. However, it is exactly with this unstated reason that the critical controversy of the argument rests, and whoever wishes to draw the conclusion into doubt must attack that assumption.

Induction

Inductive reasoning relies on data from our experience and works on the assumption that unobserved cases are likely to resemble earlier observed cases. Inductive arguments tend to be strong or weak, rather than true or false. Bertrand Russell tells the memorable tale of the inductivist turkey. This scientifically minded fowl has decided to gather data about her own life. Every day, as she is fed at 8 o'clock, she checks the great barn clock and makes a note. Eventually she believes she has sufficient data to advance the theory 'every day at eight I get fed'. She then makes the appropriate prediction: 'Tomorrow I will get fed at eight.' Unfortunately, the following day is Christmas Day.

Deduction

A deductive argument relies on pure logic. It is a form of reasoning whereby if the reasons are true, the conclusion must necessarily also be true. Consider the following argument: 'Horus is taller than Osiris, and Osiris is taller than Isis, therefore Horus is taller than Isis.' If we accept that Horus is taller than Osiris and Osiris taller than Isis, we are forced to accept that Horus is taller than Isis. Syllogisms are simple three-step deductive arguments, composed of two reasons leading to a conclusion. The most famous example is this: 'All men are mortal. Socrates is a man. Therefore, Socrates is mortal.'

Soundness

Deductive arguments must be both valid and sound. They are valid if the logic is intact, but that does not make them true. For instance, the syllogism 'All cows are pink. Nelly is a cow. Therefore, Nelly is pink,' is valid, but not sound, because, well, cows aren't pink. So even if we are given a valid argument, we must still be careful before we accept the conclusion, since a valid argument might contain a false premise.

Fallacy

Fallacies are arguments gone wrong, flawed pieces of reasoning. They can be flawed because the reasons aren't acceptable or because they don't support the conclusion. Fallacious arguments should not be persuasive, but they too often are. Fallacies may be created unintentionally, or they may be created intentionally in order to deceive other people. For example: 'You are either with us or against us' is a fallacy because it presents us with a false dichotomy, denying us the possibility of other options.

Relevance

For reasons to be properly connected to the conclusion, they must first of all be relevant to the conclusion. This means they must provide evidence in favour of the conclusion. This might sound obvious, but fallacies of relevance happen easily. For instance, in order to support their conclusions, people often make appeals to tradition, popular opinion or authority. Often, these appeals are irrelevant. For example, we might decide that ethical consumerism matters because some Hollywood actors say so, or that pacifism is a good idea because Einstein advocated it.

Is-Ought Fallacy

Hume's Law says that you cannot derive 'ought' from 'is'; in other words, factual premises cannot entail an evaluative conclusion. David Hume points out that there is a logical gap between facts and values. For example, it would be fallacious to argue that it's all right to cheat in exams because everybody does it, or that it's all right to cheat on your sexual partner because nature has equipped us to have many different partners.

Ad Hominem

Ad hominem, 'against the person', arguments aim to attack an individual or group rather than engage with their arguments. They are fallacious because on the whole they are irrelevant in a debate. It does not matter who the person is, but what they say and how good their reasoning is. If a person makes an argument against the death penalty and you happen to know that their brother has been convicted of murder, it is not good enough to say, 'Well, you would say that, wouldn't you?' No matter what their personal motivation for making the argument, it is still incumbent on you to engage with their reasons.

Analogy

Arguments by analogy are inductive arguments that rely on a comparison between two things that are alike in one or more respects. The strength of an argument by analogy relies on the quality of the comparison. The analogy breaks down when we take it too far and we assume that the two things we are comparing are alike in some respect that they are not. In that case, arguments by analogy are fallacies. Here is an example: 'Swimming is basically like dancing; both are based on good physical coordination and regular movement patterns. Since I taught myself to dance really well, I can probably teach myself to swim.'

Slippery Slope

A slippery slope is a fallacious application of conditional, 'if–then', structures, a series of less and less likely conclusions drawn from an initial statement. The trick is to know that this progression is not a necessary one. For example, 'You should never play computer games. Once you start playing you will find it hard to stop. Soon you are spending all your time playing games, and eventually you will lose your friends and perhaps even your job.' Although the dangers of gaming addiction are serious, it is possible to enjoy games once in a while without becoming addicted and ruining one's life.

Cognitive Bias

Although philosophers put all their energy and faith into sound reasoning, there is a phenomenon that throws a distinct spanner in the works of this smooth process: cognitive bias. Although nobody is excused from being rational, since everybody can be, there are habits of thinking that tempt us to leave reason by the wayside. Cognitive biases appeal to us because they are shortcuts, less time-consuming and irksome than critical analysis, allowing us to consistently vindicate long-held values and world views. Confirmation bias, for instance, is the habit of giving more attention and credence to arguments that endorse our beliefs, rather than judging all arguments on their merits, regardless of their conclusion.

Paradox

W.V.O. Quine explains that some arguments 'produce a self-contradiction by accepted ways of reasoning'. These are logical paradoxes. The classical Greek thinker Eubulides was the originator of the Liar paradox, among others. A man says: 'What I am saying now is a lie.' If this is true, it is a lie, and if it is a lie it is true. Bertrand Russell's paradox has to do with set theory and was illustrated by him as the 'barber paradox'. There is a barber 'who shaves all those, and those only, who do not shave themselves'. So, does the barber shave himself?

Definition

Giving a definition means stating necessary and sufficient conditions. For example, 'what is a grandmother?' translates into 'what are the necessary and sufficient conditions of X's being a grandmother?' Necessary conditions are those that simply must be in place for X to be a grandmother, such as having grandchildren. However, having grandchildren is not a sufficient condition for being a grandmother, since the same applies to grandfathers. Definitions can often be parts of arguments, so we must pay attention to definitions that may be vague, emotive, too narrow or too wide.

Language

Nobody can deny that many problems could be avoided if we paid more attention to language. Many philosophers go a lot further. They argue that philosophical problems can be solved either by using a language better suited to distinguishing between truth and falsehood, an ideal logical language, or by understanding our everyday language better. How does language convey meaning? Ludwig Wittgenstein in his early philosophy believed that meaning had to be injected into language from outside it. In his later philosophy, he believed that the way we use language gives it 'life'.

Rhetoric

In Martin Luther King's famous 'I have a dream' speech, all elements of great rhetoric are combined and masterfully executed. King did not simply deliver the speech; he embodied it. Rhetoric has been of interest to philosophers because the ability to convince has an important place in the political and legal contexts that determine our lives. Aristotle defines the three pillars of rhetoric – 'ethos', 'logos' and 'pathos' – respectively as being perceived as trustworthy, offering sound arguments and inspiring certain emotions in the audience. Whereas Aristotle puts a definite emphasis on good critical argumentation, the great orator and thinker Cicero argues that nothing is more powerful than a successful manipulation of the emotions.

Communication

Max is giving Audrey a lift on his new motorbike. 'Slow down!' she shouts. Max is annoyed because he feels patronized. It is a very simple situation yet one beset with numerous possibilities for miscommunicating, since 'slow down!' can carry many different connotations. Communicating well is always difficult and requires us to navigate a minefield of different concerns. Jürgen Habermas's complex system of 'communicative action' requires us to use language well but also to be honest about facts, and to avoid misconceptions both about the social world, which affects the communicative context, and about the subjective world of emotions, desires and intentions.

Language Games

Are you good at playing chess? Do you know how to play poker? Do you enjoy football? Language games are like most other games in that they have rules and are always shared with others. However, a language game is more than a pastime, it is a 'form of life'. Ludwig Wittgenstein says that language games consist 'of language and the actions into which it is woven'. Once you know the rules of the game, you can learn to play it competently. For example, to play the language game of a traditional English tea party you need the appropriate vocabulary and conversation topics as well as an understanding of polite behaviour. The more you play, the better you get.

Lie

Rachel tells Monica that there aren't any biscuits left, but actually there is a new pack at the back of the cupboard. Did Rachel lie? Not necessarily. It could be that she didn't know about the biscuits, and didn't mean to deceive Monica. For a lie to be a lie, it must be told to someone with the intention of deceiving them. A lie doesn't even have to contain an untruth. Concerned about his friend's expanding girth, Joey tells Ross the ice-cream van has run out of ice cream, although he believes this not to be true. Coincidentally, it is true, but Joey has still lied to Ross.

Metaphor

Metaphors perplex philosophers, perhaps because they do something irrational. They use a word or phrase to refer to an object to which they are not literally applicable. While some metaphors are literally true, such as John Donne's dictum that 'no man is an island', most are not; Shakespeare's Juliet is not in fact the sun, Bob Dylan is not actually friends with chaos and we are not really all in the same boat. In that sense, metaphors are a kind of lie. Yet they are everywhere, and philosophers ask why and how they work and if there is anything wrong with them, such as whether they are more manipulative than other uses of language.

Hermeneutics

Are you sometimes puzzled by Shakespeare or confused by legal contracts? Join the club. Thinkers struggling to find the correct interpretation of biblical or legal texts, of historical testimony or poetry, began to think about what 'understanding' involves. The resulting discipline of hermeneutics is aptly named after the Greek god Hermes, who not only had to physically deliver messages for the gods, but also, more challengingly, translate these messages from the language of the gods into language that humans could understand. Philosophers such as Hans-Georg Gadamer ask what the chances are of us ever truly understanding each other and if, perhaps, all understanding is in fact interpretation.

Good
& Bad

Ethics

Theorizing about what we should do and what kind of people we should be is part of the field of ethics. Here we ask questions about human morality, moral statements or claims, moral character and, perhaps most importantly, moral actions. What should I do? What kind of person should I be? How should I make decisions?

Morality

Even professional philosophers sometimes use the concepts of 'ethics' and 'morality' as if they were interchangeable. Should you come across someone who does, feel free to use the considerable authority of this book to smack them down. While ethics is a field of systematic enquiry, morality is a quality of our actions and everyday decisions. In this case 'moral' means 'morally good'; people or actions can be either moral or immoral. However, a problem is either a moral problem or a non-moral, 'amoral', problem when it involves responsibility.

Good

There are almost as many meanings of 'good' as there are contexts in which it appears: a good breakfast, a good dog, a good deed, a good friend. Philosophers pay careful attention to the way in which the word 'good' is used. George Edward Moore argues that we cannot define the word by stating natural properties; for example, we cannot say 'good is what is pleasant'. We should decide intuitively in any given situation what is good, rather than defining it universally. Otherwise, we can question each definition of 'good' with respect to its actual goodness, and what its value is and if it brings with it a moral obligation.

Evil

'Evil' makes sense only in the context of its opposite, 'good'. Traditionally, evil is seen as the deprivation of some good that is owed. The term expresses the experience of hindrances to living our lives, the denial of happiness and well-being. Buddhist philosophy says that at the centre of evil is human ignorance, from which spring greed and aggression. Together, these three are seen as the root causes of all evil in the world. Do you agree that evil comes from ignorance and that, if we could avoid greed and aggression, we could put an end to evil?

Motivation

Why do we do what we do? What makes me follow one particular course of action rather than another? A reason for action is a reason that motivates me to comply with it. What might these reasons look like? If I think 'It is good to give to charity', will this belief be enough to make me give to charity? David Hume did not think so. He maintains that 'morals excite passions, and produce or prevent actions'. According to Hume, there are two motivating factors: beliefs and desires. Only desires, however, are intrinsically motivating, whereas beliefs motivate us only if they are combined with an independent desire.

Moral Dilemma

What if sometimes there simply isn't a good answer to a moral problem? What if whatever you choose, you are not doing the right thing? What if you are forced to choose between two evils? Imagine there are two lifeboats drifting on the ocean, each containing ten people. The sea is rough and both boats are in peril. In the time it will take you to reach one boat, the other is likely to sink. Whichever way you turn, ten people will die. Such examples can show the limits of ethics, since it can offer us no way to make the decision; there is no 'good' choice.

Doing Nothing

Wu wei, 'doing nothing', is an idea that goes back to Confucius but is very prominent in classical Daoism. It describes the natural course of all things in the world. 'The Dao constantly does nothing yet nothing remains undone,' explains Laozi. We should emulate this approach to action, Daoism suggests. However, this is not a recommendation to inaction. 'Doing nothing' simply implies not forcing things, not attempting to bend circumstances to your will but spontaneously acting appropriately in any given situation.

Boo-Hurrah

What do you mean when you say 'X is good' or 'X is bad'? Emotivism – also called the 'boo-hurrah theory' – says that moral judgements are nothing but expressions of feelings of approval or disapproval. So, when you say 'it is good to help people in need' or 'it is bad to exploit the vulnerable', all you are really expressing is 'hurrah for helping people in need' or 'boo to exploiting the vulnerable'. Is that all there is to our moral judgements?

Responsibility

Why do we blame people when they have done something wrong? The answer seems obvious: because we think they are responsible for their actions. This makes sense if we assume that people are free to choose. Tom could have chosen to spend time with Jack instead of Jill; Moira could have given the money she spent on her new jacket to the homeless person outside the boutique; Julius Caesar could have decided not to cross the Rubicon.

Deontology

Deontologists such as Immanuel Kant believe that good moral choices come from good intentions based on a long-term commitment to moral principles. Being generally committed to being helpful, Greta wants to help her friend move house. Her intention is what matters. If Greta is run over by a bus before she can get there, she is not to blame. Conversely, it is possible to do some good without intending it. The billionaire Jeremy Midas might give lots of money to charity, but only because it creates tax advantages and because he likes to be called a 'philanthropist'. Although a good cause will benefit, according to deontology Midas is not morally praiseworthy. You can do the right thing for the wrong reasons.

Categorical Imperative

Immanuel Kant argued that free agents will make up their minds about moral values independent of specific situations in which they find themselves. But how do we decide what is right if we don't have a particular moral problem to solve? Kant offers a method that he believed to be neutral and rational. He called it the categorical imperative. According to this, we should adopt only principles or values that we would like to be universally valid and that respect all human beings as individuals. The commitment to not lying is a good example.

Consequentialism

What makes my action a good action? Consequentialists argue that it is good outcomes rather than good intentions that matter. What we really want to achieve by acting morally is to do some good in the world. However, if good consequences are the hallmark of a good action, we need to know which consequences are to count as good. Consequentialists differ in their answers to this question. Peter Singer believes we should always act so as to reduce suffering. This obligation leads him, for instance, to the claim that posits that all citizens of rich nations ought to give at least some of their disposable income to charities that help to alleviate poverty worldwide.

Utilitarianism

What could be more important than happiness? The prominent social reformers Jeremy Bentham and John Stuart Mill defined classical utilitarianism. Their consequentialist moral and social theory holds that utility, that is to say the degree to which an action promotes general happiness, should be the guiding consideration for moral and political action. We should act on the 'greatest happiness principle', which says that a good action is one that maximizes general happiness or minimizes pain. There are a number of problems when we try to put this into practice, such as the question of how we can measure happiness or compare the happiness of one individual to that of another.

Virtue

Virtue ethicists believe that in order to act morally we must cultivate a moral character. Virtue ethics is therefore mainly concerned not with actions but with personhood. Instead of asking the question 'What should I do?', virtue ethicists such as Confucius ask the question 'What kind of person should I be?' They believe that good actions come from good people. What we need to do is cultivate character properties that we like and, with plenty of practice, make ourselves into the person we truly think we should be. We will then act in accordance with this moral character. Aristotle promises a bonus: if we are successful, the result is well-being, a fulfilled life.

Moral Clients

Philosophers refer to those who make free decisions about their actions as 'moral agents', and to those who are affected by these actions as 'moral clients'. All rational beings are generally regarded as moral agents, whereas the class of moral clients is much larger. It includes all moral agents, as well as animals and even future generations. Perhaps we are also moral clients to ourselves? Are we morally obliged to do things for ourselves? Another case of controversial moral clientele is the environment. While it makes sense that we should treat the environment with care, trees and mountains cannot suffer. So, perhaps our moral clients are other people, animals and future generations of humans.

Bad Faith

Bad faith is a form of self-deception. It seems puzzling; why would anyone want to deceive themselves? Existentialists such as Jean-Paul Sartre believe that we are often tempted to misrepresent to ourselves what options are open to us and what are the conditions that define these options, to avoid having to make difficult decisions and consider undesirable possibilities. We either deny that we are free to choose when we are, or, conversely, make ourselves believe we have more options than is the case. For example, someone trapped in an abusive relationship might say: 'I don't like it but I can't get out.' What they really mean is that it would be very difficult to get out of the relationship, and the economic, psychological or social cost might be too great. Nonetheless, Sartre would say, it remains an option.

Hedonism

Aristippus the Elder was an incorrigible party animal and an outright defender of the unrestrained pursuit of pleasure. He seems to have been the paradigmatic hedonist, valuing pleasure above all else. However, most hedonists have been more subtle. Epicurus imagined pleasure and pain to be on the same spectrum, and believed a rather ascetic lifestyle to be the best policy for a good life. Being a thoughtful hedonist, he realized that not all pleasures are choice-worthy or all pains to be avoided. Pleasures can turn into pains and pains can turn into pleasures. For example, it may be wise to bear the pain of exam stress for the sake of an educational degree, but to forgo the pleasure of regular cream cakes in order to avoid the pain of diabetes or obesity.

Integrity

A person of integrity is easy to get along with. There are no nasty surprises, and you know what they stand for. Integrity means that a person's actions reflect their beliefs, values and ideals. So, if Tom is a pacifist, you know he won't beat you up. Harry Frankfurt explains the process of exercising integrity as that of making choices between conflicting desires. Integrity, then, means choosing the right desire. It is in this process, Frankfurt believes, that we 'constitute' ourselves.

Moral Luck

Imagine two possible scenarios. Will and Karen are standing on the roof of a building hauling a piano up to the third floor. In their haste, they didn't pay much attention to safety and only used a single, poorly attached rope, but the piano arrives safely in its intended location. Now imagine instead that the insufficiently secured piano slips and crashes down onto the pavement below, squashing the neighbour's cat. Bernard Williams calls this a case of 'moral luck', because we will blame Will and Karen severely if the piano causes an accident but not if it doesn't. This, strangely, means that their moral blameworthiness depends on circumstances beyond their control. The problem of moral luck has many real-life applications, from drink-driving to health and safety in the workplace.

Supererogatory

No matter how much good you do in the world, is it ever enough? How many spectacular birthday parties do you have to organize for your child? To how many charities must you regularly donate? Are we ever justified in doing things for ourselves while others are suffering? A supererogatory act is morally good and goes beyond what is required by duty. Some moral theories, such as utilitarianism, that demand that we always act in the interests of maximizing moral outcomes cannot accommodate supererogatory acts.

Shame

Shame, Jean-Paul Sartre explains, is a deeply human emotion. It is also a particularly unpleasant experience, since it cuts right to the core of our being. Sartre believed that we are never just ashamed of *something*, but that, in shame, we are ultimately ashamed of *what we are*. Shame, in contrast to guilt, is social. It comes from the thought of what we are in the eyes of others. It is also not always about morally pivotal matters; Holly might be ashamed of having forgotten to put a stamp on a letter she posted, simply because she is worried the receiver will think less of her. Shame can even set in when nobody will ever find out what we do. Frank can be ashamed of not having brushed his teeth simply by thinking about what his mother might have said if she had known.

Regret

Well, you did it. You were not supposed to do it, but you could not help yourself. Selfishly, you scoffed the last of your housemate's biscuits. Now you are feeling bad. Does it matter what we feel when we have transgressed against our moral commitments? Philippa Foot argues that regret does not make any difference to the situation. Therefore, regret is irrational. However, it teaches you not to get into the same kind of situation again, if you can avoid it.

Relativism

Are human rights morally binding in some societies but misconceived in others? Is slavery morally wrong today but was it perhaps not in the past? Relativism is the claim that there is more than one truth. A famous formulation of relativism is that made by the ancient Greek sophist Protagoras: 'Man is the measure of all things.' Moral relativism is the view that moral standards are rooted in social custom, and therefore vary from one culture to another and from one era to another. Some argue that relativism is needed for tolerance. However, the opposite is true; tolerance is needed not if everybody is right, but only if you think the other is wrong.

Egoism

At the end of the philosophy class, Mindy realizes it's raining hard outside. She spots Phil's umbrella in the corner and decides to use it, intending to return it at the following meeting. She reasons that one of them will get wet, so why should it be her and not Phil? The belief that all human actions are ultimately motivated by selfish or egoistic inclinations is called psychological egoism. Thomas Hobbes takes this view of human nature. He is also a moral egoist, believing that egoism is a good thing since we will realize that our self-interest in the long term is best served by cooperating with others. In this way, selfishness leads to moral behaviour.

Altruism

Do we ever act altruistically? Do we do things just for others? Sometimes it clearly feels like it. Instead of going to see the new Star Wars movie, Quentin has decided to visit his Aunt Nellie in hospital. Since there is no doubt in his mind that he would have preferred the former over the latter, he may feel good about himself in the knowledge that, because he is doing this for her, he is acting altruistically. However, it is possible that he was negatively motivated by the fact that he would have felt guilty if he had chosen his pleasure over her need. In this way it is difficult to think of any act that is truly altruistic.

Friendship

What is so good about friends? They can clearly be fun as well as useful; they will be good company on a night out and may water your plants while you're on holiday. To Aristotle, however, this does not even scratch the surface. He thought that our friends can bring out the best in us and help us become the best we can be. This is because friendship is also a challenge; it is not easy to be a good friend to others and to be deserving of their friendship in return. Rising to this challenge will make you both good and happy.

Effective Giving

The new movement of effective altruism is based on the philosophy of Peter Singer, who argues that not only can we act altruistically, we are morally required to do so. The existence in the world of evils such as extreme poverty means that everybody who can help must do so. Singer, who gives a third of his income to charity, explains that effective altruism means we ought to practise 'effective giving': giving not randomly but in such a way that the resources – time or money – we give will have the greatest possible positive effect in the world. In order to encourage others to join this project, Singer suggests fostering a 'culture of giving'.

Realism

Is the world a value-free environment of physical facts?
Are moral responses simply an add-on? Do we project
them into the world? Our experience sometimes seems
to indicate otherwise. It simply does not tie in with the
complexity of human existence that fact and value,
although conceptually separable, are also separate
in real life. So when I see a person who has just been
knocked off her bike by a speeding car lying bleeding
by the roadside, this clearly is a situation full of pain,
anger and injustice, challenging me to respond with
sympathy, care and concern. Moral realists would say
that these are moral facts.

Ambiguity

Hugo has plans for travelling in order to vlog to
YouTube audiences about environmental concerns
from remote places. However, there are too many
obstacles to overcome – economic, administrative and
technical. What is he to do? Simone de Beauvoir's *Ethics
of Ambiguity* locates human existence in a half-world
between our mental freedom to choose projects and the
heaviness of the world, which can weigh us down and
prevent us from realizing those projects. She believed
that to live a good life, rather than evade it, we must face
and embrace this ambiguity. The only way of realizing
our projects, she reveals, lies in inviting others to join
them freely. So, if Hugo can enthuse others, he will

be able to overcome real-world difficulties with their support. The only way of living a satisfactory life is in positive cooperation with others.

Contributory Causation

What difference does it make if I recycle, give blood, vote? My contribution is so tiny, it doesn't seem to matter. Jonathan Glover uses the following story to show that this is a fallacy. Every day, 100 poor villagers are robbed by 100 bandits of their only meal of 100 beans each, as each bandit takes one villager's meal from them. One day the bandits begin to feel guilty about robbing the poor. So, instead of each taking the entire meal of one villager, each bandit now takes only one bean from every villager's bowl. Surely, the loss of one bean doesn't make a noticeable difference, so no bandit will have harmed anyone.

Ethical Consumerism

When Socrates took a walk through a busy marketplace
with a wealth of goods on offer, he remarked: 'It's
surprising how many things there are that I don't need.'
Consumerism is a big problem in our time, and in recent
years ethical consumerism has become a point of public
discussion. It means adapting our shopping habits
to moral ends with the aim of reducing our negative
impact on people, animals and the environment. It
makes shopping a complex topic, from being mindful
of packaging materials to fair-trade conditions, and
animal welfare to political and social injustice.

Meaning
& Purpose

Meaning

How can we find meaning in life? Perhaps life is like
a treasure hunt and the world like a large puzzle.
If we can figure it out, meaning will reveal itself.
Perhaps we have to create our own meaning. Søren
Kierkegaard describes three stages of life, each with its
own meaning. In the aesthetic stage we find fulfilment
in sense experience, in art, dance or skydiving. The
ethical stage is one when meaning comes from working
towards moral aims and causes. The highest stage is
the religious stage, when we single-mindedly commit
ourselves to a set of values. To do this, we must perform
a 'leap of faith', since we cannot know if we are choosing
the right thing. This risk adds value to our choice.

Absurdity

Albert Camus recounts for us the story of Sisyphus,
the hero in Greek mythology who, condemned to
punishment by the gods, had to heave a large boulder
eternally up a slope. Once at the top, he would have
to watch the boulder roll back down, then restart
the process. Are our lives like this? The world is not
arranged for our comfort; it does not cooperate with
our thoughts, hopes and desires. Camus tells us that
we must face absurdity head on. He associates this
spirit of rebellion with the Greek hero Prometheus,
who stole fire from the gods: own the absurdity of
your life instead of being a victim.

Function

Do human beings have a function? Machines clearly do, but people seem very different. Aristotle, however, believed that all things had a purpose, including humans. For anything with a function, doing the right thing means fulfilling the function. That which has a function is itself considered good if it fulfils its function well. For example, it is the function of a knife to cut things. If it cuts well, it is a good knife. Humans are not much different. Aristotle believed the function of the human soul was to act according to reason. If this function is performed well, the result is excellence and the person is virtuous.

Value

What do you value and why do you value it? Aristotle distinguishes different kinds of good thing. We value 'instrumental goods' not for their own sake but as a means to some other end. Money is an example. It is not valuable in itself but enables us to obtain things that we value. 'Ultimate goods' are valuable in themselves. They are the most worthwhile pursuing. A small class of things are valuable both in themselves *and* instrumentally. Health is such a thing. It is simply good to be healthy, but it is also good from the point of view of anything else you might want to do.

Culture

As human beings, we inhabit a world that is of our own making. A culture is a 'life-world', a context in which we live and act, defined by a set of beliefs, ideas, attitudes, values and practices accepted by a group or organization. The more of these that are shared, the stronger the culture. Culture does not just affect fashion, art or lifestyle trends; it also has an impact on how we conduct political discourse, think about morality and make important decisions. Max Horkheimer and Theodor Adorno believed that for the majority of people this is not a free process. They warned that culture has become an alluring but dangerous 'industry' of 'mass deception'.

Pleasure

Pleasure is better than pain; that much seems obvious. But it is a difficult word to pin down, since pleasure comes in many different forms. The pleasure of a cup of hot cocoa on a cold day is very different from the pleasure of your grandchild being born or the pleasure of a picnic on the beach. Hedonists claim that pleasure is always good, but clearly the objects of pleasure are not. Some people take pleasure in terrible things, such as the misfortune or suffering of others. The pursuit of pleasure at that cost is illegitimate. Any philosophy that aims to allot pleasure a prominent place must find a way of making such distinctions.

Happiness

One of the best texts on happiness is Epicurus' short 'Letter to Menoeceus'. Epicurus gives us a few simple arguments and practical hints about how to be happy. He learns from Aristotle that happiness comes from human actions rather than luck, and is independent of wealth and status. However, while Epicurus valued pleasure, Aristotle believed true happiness to come from being a moral person. He called this quality of happiness *eudaimonia*, which is sometimes translated as 'human flourishing'. *Eudaimonia* is not a 'pop the champagne corks' kind of happiness but a sense of well-being that comes from knowing that you are the best you can be and from acting accordingly.

Work

When Karl Marx talks about how human beings work in order to survive, he attributes great importance to their productive activity: 'It is ... a definite form of expressing their life, a definite mode of life on their part. As individuals express their life, so they are. What they are, therefore, coincides with their production, both with what they produce and with how they produce.' As humans we are therefore defined by what we do and create. It is for this reason that Marx emphasizes how important it is for us to work under the right conditions, conditions that give us the freedom to be creative, to be fully human.

Religion

Sets of beliefs, values and life choices, often with a core element that can be described as spiritual, shared by a community can be called 'religions', although there really is not a good enough definition. John Hick uses a parable to show how religion can make a difference to our lives. Two men are travelling together along a road. One of them believes that it leads to the Celestial City, the other that it leads nowhere, but it is the only road. On the way they experience moments of happiness, but also obstacles and danger. One of them interprets the good parts of the journey as rewards and the bad ones as trials of his purpose. The other simply enjoys the good and endures the bad. Hick's point is that the believer disagrees with the atheist about the meaning of life.

Love

In his eloquent dialogue *The Symposium*, Plato describes a drinking party at which the participants discuss love. The different thinkers come up with a variety of definitions of love, covering both friendship, *philia*, and romantic love, *eros*. The most memorable among them is Aristophanes' account. He tells us about a fictional past in which humans were so perfect that Zeus in jealous anger cut each person in half, with the result that we are no longer complete and must spend our time looking for our other half. Love finds many other applications in philosophy. It can be a framework for moral activity. Augustine tells

us: 'Love and do what you will.' As long as your base
attitude is that of goodwill and love for others, your
actions will not be far off the moral mark.

God

Does perfection exist? Plato describes God as 'perfect
in all respects', and Aristotle introduces the idea of God
as 'unmoved mover' and 'final cause'. God features in
many ways in the history of philosophy. An important
connection is that between God and morality. Is
morality without God possible? As Fyodor Dostoevsky's
Grand Inquisitor states so clearly: 'If God is dead
everything is permitted.' In one of the most explosive
texts in the history of philosophy, Friedrich Nietzsche
claims that just this has come to pass – 'God is dead' –
and, what is worse, 'we have killed him'. Is this possible?

Atheism

Is there a God? Atheists generally deny the existence
of a deity, although there are many different forms of
atheism. Ludwig Feuerbach believed faith and religion
to be mistakes. He also thought they had harmful effects
on our common lives, since we waste so much of our
love on God, a non-existing entity, instead of using it
to enrich our human relationships. Karl Marx famously
claimed that religion is 'the opium of the masses', that
religion acts as a painkiller to make our lives bearable.

Miracles

Are miracles possible? David Hume defines a miracle as 'a transgression of a law of nature by a particular volition of the Deity, or by the interposition of some invisible agent'. What evidence supports the occurrence of miracles? There are usually only a few witnesses, so we must think about the reliability of their testimony. Hume recommends comparing the likelihood of the miracle occurring with the likelihood of the witnesses being mistaken. We will always find the latter less improbable than the former. Belief in miracles is motivated by interest in the unusual or by faith, where the believer will experience 'a continued miracle in his own person, which subverts all the principles of his understanding'.

Nihilism

Nihilists deny the existence of aspects of reality, of a moral law, truth, beauty or other values. Nihilism gets bad press, but some forms can be interesting. It is a position that allows us to be critical of assumptions of meaning, value and even the status of rationality. Friedrich Nietzsche, for example, opposed the view that the world was in itself structured or organized; he said that only human minds can impose order on the world. 'Every belief, every considering something-true,' he claims, 'is necessarily false because there is simply no true world.'

Human Condition

All that can be said in universal terms about human existence is that all human beings share in a particular set of conditions that surround their being. This is what Jean-Paul Sartre calls the Human Condition. The following aspects define the Human Condition: being in the world, dealing with the world, being with others, being free and being mortal. No human being can escape having to live by these rules. To be able to make the most of our lives, we must face up to having to make responsible choices in light of these conditions.

Individualism

While other people are unavoidable in any human life, some philosophers emphasize that any human life is fundamentally the life of an individual and that we are on our own. In order to be realistic about life, we must face this isolation. Martin Heidegger suggests that in order to do so we should remind ourselves regularly of our own mortality, since death is the one event in life that we clearly face on our own. To other thinkers, individualism is less difficult and more promising, giving us the opportunity to mould our lives the way we see fit.

The Other

'Hell is other people,' declares a character in Jean-Paul Sartre's play *No Exit*. It sums up what Sartre explains in his philosophy concerning the existence of others. Living with other people is inescapable in a human life. Even if you decide to avoid their company and live as a hermit, you do so in response to their presence. Sartre believed that the other transforms our world, as we worry about the judgement of others and suffer from the obstacles they put in our way.

Individuals & Society

Politics

According to Harold Lasswell, politics is about 'who gets what, when and how'. This approach works well for philosophers. Politics is the context in which we need to decide who gets which resources, incomes, opportunities, privileges, rights, immunities or punishments, and who gets to decide all that in the first place. Politics, therefore, defines the conditions for our common life. It is a matter of perspective if the emphasis should be on the protection of the individual against the multitude or on the greatest possible integration of the individual into the group.

Justice

Once I asked a class to come up with basic principles of justice. By the end of the session the only thing everybody could agree on was 'no parking tickets'. John Rawls, however, believes that people would make constructive decisions on fundamental principles for a society if they knew they had to live in it but didn't yet know if they would be at the top or bottom of the social spectrum. He believes they would want to ensure that each individual enjoys 'the most extensive basic liberty' possible, has access to 'offices and positions open to all under conditions of fair equality of opportunity' and will receive support if they are one of the 'least advantaged'.

Power

Niccolò Machiavelli believes a ruler, a 'prince', needs special personal qualities if they are to hold on to power. Political power is connected to political agency and, to him, means the ability to stay in charge and 'achieve great things'. A ruler must be effective, a fighter and good at getting things done. It is not important for the prince to be a good person. On the contrary, they should be prepared to do anything necessary to stay in power, even resort to cruelty if it is 'well used'. Although the prince must not incur the hatred of his subjects, since that might destabilize his position, it is better to be feared than to be popular, since this is the way a strong sense of political obligation is created in the population.

Communitarianism

What matters more, society or the individual? Aristotle thinks we are naturally at home in communities, and describes humans as 'political animals'. Charles Taylor goes further by decrying 'individualism' as one of the 'malaises of modernity'. While it is good for a person to think about their own life, there is a 'dark side of individualism'. It often makes us focus on ourselves in a way that denies or underestimates the contexts that give human life meaning and significance. We think of ourselves as isolated, but as we try to find ourselves, we find nothing, unless we recognize that we are social and historical beings.

State

Thomas Hobbes lived during the English Civil War. It taught him that there is nothing worse than the absence of political order, a situation where life is 'nasty, brutish and short'. The state is the solution: a human-made entity, involving a sovereign ruling over subjects. Its function is to relieve people of the great insecurity that rules their lives without it: 'For by Art is created a great Leviathan called Common-Wealth, or State ... which is but an Artificial Man; though of greater stature and strength than the Naturall, for whose protection and defence it was intended.' Note that Hobbes refers to the state as a 'Leviathan', a kind of monster. Politics brings no paradise, just the lesser of two evils.

Political Obligation

Jules Verne's Captain Nemo despises governments. Living in his luxurious submarine allows him to evade political authority: 'God, if he believed in Him, and his conscience, if he had one, were the only judges to whom he was answerable.' Most of us do not have that option. Living in a political state means accepting political obligation – if the government is legitimate. Legal obligation, a subcategory of political obligation, requires us to abide by the law. However, it is widely agreed that injustice or violence on the part of the state cancel out this obligation.

Voluntarism

Do we freely consent to the political arrangements that affect our lives? Political voluntarism assures us that a person is subject to political authority only if she has freely consented to it. John Locke shares that assumption. Now he has to show how someone can give the state its authority over them. Locke thinks we 'tacitly' consent to the state simply by living there. David Hume disagrees; he says tacit consent is like waking up on a ship in the middle of the ocean, forced either to do whatever the captain demands or jump ship. The only way of withholding tacit political consent would be to leave the country.

Punishment

Michel Foucault suggests that punishment in a traditional sense – the use of violence and executions – has been superseded by 'discipline'. The idea is 'to punish less, perhaps; but certainly to punish better'. Disciplinary power has three elements: hierarchical observation, normalizing judgement and examination. The point of discipline is to turn individuals into 'docile bodies', easily controlled by just observing them. Prisons are laid out in ways that facilitate monitoring, but so are public spaces, sports arenas and schools. Our lives are structured accordingly, and cameras abound.

Civil Disobedience

Do we have rights against our governments? The idea of 'civil disobedience' suggests that we do. It was coined by Henry David Thoreau. He refused to pay the state poll tax, which supported a war in Mexico as well as the enforcement of the Fugitive Slave Law, to signal his moral disapproval of both policies: 'If the injustice ... is of such a nature that it requires you to be the agent of injustice to another, then I say, break the law. Let your life be a counter-friction to stop the machine. What I have to do is to see, at any rate, that I do not lend myself to the wrong which I condemn.'

Social Contract

How can we best describe society? According to social contract theories, we are bound to others by a contract. There are different possible configurations of this arrangement. In Thomas Hobbes's version, the contract is between citizens but excludes the sovereign, who is above the contract. The sovereign has obligations *with respect to* her subjects but not *to* her subjects. This is like me promising your grandmother that I will buy you an ice cream; I have an obligation *with respect to* you but *to* your grandmother.

Liberty

'Man is born free, but he is everywhere in chains,' laments Jean-Jacques Rousseau. Liberty – political freedom – is a precious commodity. John Stuart Mill warned that we must understand that the traditional idea of liberty, meaning 'protection against the tyranny of political rulers', had become inadequate, and that in modern democracies we must be wary of the 'tyranny of the majority'. It is fine to argue with a person about their choices, but not to force them: 'Over himself, over his own body and mind, the individual is sovereign.'

Equality

In Jorge Luis Borges's story 'The Lottery in Babylon', he imagines a society where the fortunes of all citizens are decided by a regular draw. You can win not only cash prizes but also fame, rights, power, imprisonment, even mutilation and execution. It sounds like an utterly absurd arrangement. Everything that happens to the citizens of Babylon is divorced from their actions: merit or guilt do not incur consequences, and rewards and punishments are random. But is there justice in this randomness? Although merit does not count, neither do economic advantage, privilege and status.

Rights

Everybody knows that having rights is a good thing, but what exactly does it mean? Rights entitle you to act without impediment from others, or place others under the obligation to do something for you. For example, my employment contract entitles me to a salary that my employer must pay. Some rights, such as this one, are legal rights. Others, such as human rights, are moral rights and, finally, there are customary rights, the weakest form of rights, which entitle you to have certain expectations based on common practices in your community, such as retirement gifts or birthday cards.

Freedom of Speech

'I disapprove of what you say, but I will defend to the death your right to say it.' This pretty much sums up what Voltaire thought about our right to express our views; he was a defender of absolute freedom of speech. In other words, there should be no restrictions at all when it comes to what people are allowed to say. After all, if it's not absolute freedom of speech, in a way it's not actually freedom of speech. On the other hand, there are plenty of examples of speech that most of us don't particularly wish to defend, for example posting instructions on how to make a bomb online, or randomly insulting a stranger.

Democracy

Democracy literally means 'rule by the people', and it contrasts with rule by one or a few. But don't too many cooks spoil the broth? Plato had his doubts about how well democracy could work. He likened it to a journey on a ship, where the captain, although competent, comes across as awkward and the travellers lose confidence in him. One by one, charming but smug passengers will volunteer to take over the helm. Since they do not understand what is involved in navigating a ship, it soon turns into a crazy journey on a ship of fools. Is democracy inefficient?

Anarchy

Do we really need a government? Some political theorists and activists deny the need for a political authority and even structure altogether. Any authority exercising political power is seen as encroaching on the political freedom of individuals. Anarchists trust in the human ability to cooperate, self-organize and resolve conflicts among themselves in a constructive way. Anarchism – theories and doctrines of anarchy – comes in very diverse forms. Some stress the importance of liberty, others emphasize mutuality; some see the individual as central, others the community; some defend private property rights, others condemn property and advocate collectivization.

Ideology

'A comfortable, smooth, reasonable, democratic unfreedom prevails in advanced industrial civilization, a token of technical progress.' Herbert Marcuse's classic *The One Dimensional Man* starts off with this haunting warning of the stealthy withdrawal of our freedom. How is this possible? The answer is: ideology, the systematic and all-embracing political discourse, which shapes politics as well as our personal life choices. The thinkers of the Frankfurt School, including Marcuse, have as their declared aim the 'criticism of ideology'. We should become aware of the features of the ideology in our lives, so that we can recover our freedom.

Dissent

John Stuart Mill is a defender of pluralism. To him, muzzling opinions is wrong because it robs 'the human race, posterity as well as the existing generation'. He gives a number of reasons why dissenting voices are important. On the one hand, the dissenter may be right or partially right, so it is worth considering their views. On the other hand, it may be that the majority or accepted view is true and the dissenter wrong. Even then, says Mill, it is important to engage with their arguments; any idea, if it is not debated, will turn into 'dead dogma', even a truth that is just held as a prejudice and no longer fully understood. It is important to allow our views to be challenged, so that we are clear about our own beliefs.

Money

Karl Marx had strong views on money. He did not like it much. Money, he believes, turns all values into their opposites. He also worries that the language of morality gets mixed up with the language of money and credit. 'What are you worth?' is a question about economic status, but sounds as though it is about the value of a person. Marx criticizes the money and credit system for being dehumanizing, as it makes us judge humans by their credit-'worthiness', contributes to economic dependence and fosters a culture of dishonesty and distrust.

Totalitarianism

Totalitarianism is a political system in which the state wields total authority and seeks to control all aspects of public and private life. Hannah Arendt's analysis shows how totalitarian regimes secure their power by indoctrination until citizens give up their freedom and individuality, joining the ruling ideology: 'Totalitarian government can be safe only to the extent that it can mobilize man's own will power in order to force him into that gigantic movement of History or Nature which supposedly uses mankind as its material and knows neither birth nor death.' The regime determines what reality is. Individuals, steeped in propaganda without alternative viewpoints, lose their ability to think outside the totalitarian box.

Nation State

Max Weber said a nation state is an entity that can 'successfully uphold a claim on the monopoly of the legitimate use of physical force within a specific territory'. Ernest Gellner puts political definition of this kind in context. In his reflections on nationalism, he comes to the conclusion that political 'nation states' must be distinguished from the 'cultural nation'. They are thought of as connected, but are often independent of each other: 'Neither nations nor states exist at all times and in all circumstances ... The state has certainly emerged without the help of the nation. Some nations have certainly emerged without the blessings of their own state.'

Nationalism

In his critical essay on 'Fatherland', Voltaire sharply condemns nationalism. He believes it to be a meaningless, fuzzy idea, although with a passionate following, mainly from those without much power or privilege in society. His main criticism is that it creates competitive divisions between citizens of different countries: 'To be a good patriot is to wish that one's city may be enriched by trade, and be powerful by arms. It is clear that ... to wish for one's country's greatness is to wish harm to one's neighbours. He who should wish that his fatherland might never be greater, smaller, richer, poorer, would be a citizen of the world.'

Cosmopolitanism

One of the most colourful figures in the history of philosophy, Diogenes the Cynic, was once asked where he came from. His answer was simply: 'I am a citizen of the world.' The Cynics believed that the good life was cosmopolitan. We should live in accordance with nature, not hesitating to depart from convention, following a universal ethics beyond the boundaries of nations or group loyalties. The Stoics agreed even more emphatically with cosmopolitanism, arguing that the whole world was already one state by virtue of being ordered by universal laws of nature, and that we should be concerned about everybody, irrespective of geography.

War

War is an intentional, large-scale armed conflict between political entities. Is such a terrible act ever justified? Perhaps we are mistaken when we think about what can be gained by war. Focusing more on the human costs of war might help us to avoid armed conflict. The feminist philosopher Sara Ruddick suggests that 'maternal thinking', a perspective open to all genders, will facilitate this. However, is there a possibility that in the right circumstances war can be just? Thomas Aquinas's theory is one of the earliest attempts to outline criteria for a just war, defining conditions both for entering a war (*jus ad bellum*) and for fighting it (*jus in bello*). Today the Geneva Convention addresses some of these concerns.

Peace

In his satirical essay 'Perpetual Peace', the title of which was taken from 'a Dutch innkeeper's sign upon which a burial ground was painted', Immanuel Kant discusses what may be seen as a fantasy, a 'sweet dream' cherished by philosophers and other optimists: the possibility of a lasting peace between nations. He believes this to be possible in principle, and outlines the precise conditions that must be in place for it to work. He believes in the necessity of sovereign states joining together freely in a strong international political structure that will outline conditions for cooperation and prevent large states from bullying small ones. All states should be 'republics', since common people will be more inclined towards peace than the privileged few.

Property

Jean-Jacques Rousseau believed the idea of private property to be at the root of inequality between humans. He describes the imaginary scenario of the first person ever to fence in a piece of land and declare it their own: 'What crimes, wars, murders, what miseries and horrors would the human race have been spared had someone pulled up the stakes or filled in the ditch and cried out to his fellow men: "Do not listen to this impostor. You are lost if you forget that the fruits of the earth belong to all and the earth to no one."'

Utopia

Utopia, 'no place', is the idea of an ideal political and social order, and allows us to explore what life would be like in a hypothetical political situation. Plato, critical of the real politics of his time, describes in detail utopian Kallipolis, the 'beautiful city'. In doing so, he discusses salient political issues such as justice, education and government. Many of his conclusions are controversial, such as his insistence on a rigid class structure and the legitimacy of fundamental political lies. Others are of serious relevance even today, such as his emphasis on education and his criticism of democracy, which lead him to suggest that philosophers should rule.

Art &
Beauty

Aesthetics

Aesthetics, although nowadays a flourishing philosophical discipline, has traditionally been the neglected stepdaughter of philosophy. However, if Immanuel Kant is right in saying that philosophy is about finding answers to the question 'What is a human being?', we would have to admit that the question cannot be adequately answered if we ignore the human ability to appreciate things from an aesthetic point of view. Our ability to make statements such as 'The rose is beautiful' is very different from saying 'The rose is red'. This gives you a first hint at how important and difficult is the study of art and beauty in philosophy.

Art

People talk about 'art' all the time, and we seem to communicate about art without any problems. However, once we try to define art, it becomes clear that this is nearly impossible. Can we really outline necessary and sufficient conditions for X being a work of art? The difficulty lies in coming up with essential criteria that will distinguish works of art from non-art, and that will include in the former all the works we wish to call 'art'. After all, the category potentially holds objects as diverse as paintings and caricatures, symphonies and lullabies, sculptures and found objects. Note that you cannot exclude anything on the grounds that you don't like it, since the question

'What is good art?' is very different from 'What is art?', and requires different criteria.

Mimesis

Surprisingly, it is Plato – the great philosopher not known for his love of art – who has provided us with the most enduring, although in modern times highly embattled, definition of art: mimesis. It is a Greek word that is often translated as 'imitation' but is perhaps best understood as 'representation'. Plato believed that all artistic creations are a kind of representation of the world of our experience. This idea holds water for many works of art, although it does not cover abstract art or include found objects. How useful is the idea of 'mimesis' today?

Beauty

Is beauty really in the eye of the beholder, or is it an objective quality? Is it primarily to be discovered in nature, or should we turn to art to find it? Many philosophers agree that there is a strong connection between beauty and pleasure, but it is difficult to define this relationship. Do we know that X is beautiful because it gives us pleasure, or does the pleasure follow from the insight that X is beautiful? George Santayana sees it this way: 'Beauty is pleasure objectified – pleasure regarded as the quality of an object.'

Sublime

Edmund Burke tells us that beauty and the sublime are mutually exclusive, and that the imagination is moved to awe and a degree of horror by what is 'dark, uncertain, and confused'. Immanuel Kant thought the sublime object was that which is 'infinitely vast or infinitely great'. The experience is one not of pleasure, as in the case of beauty, but of awe. Burke believes the sublime to be connected with pain and danger, as in thoughts of shipwrecks and desolate heathlands, resulting in 'delightful horror'. The Romantics also associated this emotion with a mixture of horror and aesthetic appreciation, as triggered for example by the sight of ruined buildings.

Expression

Expression theory tells us that the hallmark of a work of art is that it expresses. According to Leo Tolstoy, a piece of art is the expression of the feelings of the artist, capable of evoking a similar state of mind in the observer. In order for there to be genuine communication between the feelings of the artist and her audience, it is necessary for the artist to have had these feelings in the first place. Much of what is generally regarded as art must therefore be dismissed as 'counterfeit'. The clearer the communication between artist and audience – in Tolstoy's words, 'the stronger the infection' – the better the art.

Play

Friedrich Schiller believed that art could educate humanity, that it could change us profoundly as individuals and communities. He identifies two cultural extremes: we are motivated either by a 'form drive', the desire to be rational and organized, or by a 'sense drive', the desire for a variety of sense experiences. He explains that either in its pure form is detrimental. The only way to achieve balance in our personal and social lives is by engaging with art. Art triggers a third drive in us, the 'play drive', which can help us to mediate between the other two: 'Man only plays when he is in the fullest sense of the word a human being, and he is only fully a human being when he plays.'

Art World

Do you like Pop Art? It was the first art genre that made Arthur Danto ask some fundamental questions about how we should approach aesthetics. Seeing Warhol's Brillo boxes confirmed to him that we have entered a new age of aesthetic experience with a need for a new philosophical approach. He therefore suggests that we pay particular attention to the *context* of art: the community of art lovers, artists, critics, gallery owners, collectors, anyone participating in a discourse about art, as well as institutions such as galleries, museums, theatres and film festivals. All this amounts to 'an atmosphere of art theory'. This is the art world.

Institutional Theories

Maybe there is nothing that essentially makes something a work of art. More recent, 'institutional' theories therefore take a different approach. George Dickie suggests the following definition: 'A work of art is an artefact of a kind created to be presented to an artworld public.' The advantage of open theories of this kind is that they can accommodate less conventional art, such as found objects. However, Dickie's theory has been criticized on the grounds that art outside the art world must be possible. Furthermore, couldn't even the art world be mistaken?

Judgement

Immanuel Kant defines judgement as 'the ability to think the particular as contained under the universal'. He distinguishes between two different kinds of judgement, one of which is important for appreciating art and beauty. A judgement is 'determinative' if it subsumes a particular case under an *already given* universal. For example, I know that the little creature in the cage is a bird, because I already have the universal concept of 'bird' available to me. To make aesthetic judgements, however, we need 'reflective judgement'. The concept 'beauty' is not a fixed universal like 'bird'. What makes it so exciting to say 'This is beautiful' is that I have to discover the concept 'beauty' afresh every time I say it.

Ideal Critic

How can we settle disagreements about whether aesthetic judgements are subjective or objective? Can we even meaningfully disagree about this? If it is just a matter of personal like or dislike, we must agree to disagree. That is where the ideal critic comes in. David Hume suggests that there are individuals who are normal observers but have much experience in aesthetic matters, whose taste is adroit. We should be inspired by their judgement and align ours with theirs, he suggests. Hume hits the mark concerning the common-sense intuition that there is much to learn about art and that the ability to judge it competently must be cultivated. Just one problem: who is the ideal critic? If you find her, let me know.

Humour

What makes a situation or remark funny? Three theories dominate the field. Immanuel Kant's incongruity theory says that things are funny when something does not quite fit. Imagine a philosophy conference where all the eminent professors are wearing pink tutus, or a house made entirely of butter. He also believed that this is how humour enables us to deal with the unexpected. Sigmund Freud's relief theory understands humour as a mechanism for releasing tension. Finally, there is the superiority theory: 'Laughter', explains Thomas Hobbes, 'is nothing else but sudden glory arising from some sudden conception of some eminency in ourselves, by comparison with the infirmity of others, or with our own, formerly.' Is humour essentially nasty?

Music

What is a piece of music? How does it express? What makes it aesthetically valuable? How can music be 'sad' or 'happy'? Even the definition of 'music' is controversial. Jerrold Levinson talks about 'organized sound', but this is a description of speech, sirens and Morse code too. Eventually, he arrives at the following definition: music consists of 'sounds temporally organized by a person for the purpose of enriching or intensifying experience through active engagement (for example, listening, dancing, performing) with the sounds regarded primarily, or in significant measure, as sounds.'

Paradox of Fiction

Why do we feel upset at the death of Shakespeare's Cordelia, or shocked when we learn that Darth Vader is Luke's father, or worried for Little Red Riding Hood alone in the dark wood? What is wrong with us? All these are just made-up stories, after all. Having an emotion normally involves believing that whatever the emotion is about really exists, so why do we have feelings on behalf of fictional characters? A common explanation is that we *identify* with them. However, this is a flawed account, since we never actually think we are them. We never really suspend our disbelief; we always know that we are reading a book or watching a performance. So what is going on?

Tragedy

How many times have you seen *Hamlet*? Perhaps you prefer a good horror film? Real-life tragedies are clearly to be avoided; nobody wants to experience a car crash, bereavement, illness or poverty. However, in fiction we positively seek out tragedy. Why is this? Philosophers refer to it as the 'paradox of tragedy'. Tragedy is associated with pity and fear, emotions that in our everyday life are very unwelcome. David Hume believes that in a fictional context two different emotions set in. On the one hand, there is our reaction of pity and fear to the plot. However, there is also delight at the masterful form of the work, through which all negative emotions are transformed into pleasure. Is this really what happens?

Catharsis

One thing is for sure, tragedy is never good news. Terry Eagleton aptly describes the tragic as 'very sad and sometimes very *very* sad'. Sounds bad. Luckily, Aristotle promises us that tragedy in fiction will make us feel 'cleansed'. 'Tragedy,' he says, 'is an imitation of an action that is serious, complete, and of a certain magnitude ... through pity and fear effecting the proper catharsis of these emotions.' In fascinated terror you have sat through yet another production of *Oedipus Rex*. It has all ended in madness, mutilation, suicide and exile, just as you knew it would. You step out of the theatre into the cool, fresh air and take a deep breath. Feel better? This is catharsis.

Comedy

Friedrich Schiller was one of the most celebrated writers of tragedy of his time, which makes a central message in his philosophical musings on comedy slightly awkward. He tells us that comedy was a superior form of art to tragedy! The reason is that in a tragedy the plot is in itself compelling, whereas in a comedy the artistic form alone makes for the success or failure of the work. As Schiller puts it, the comic poet must be in excellent artistic control, 'at home' in his work; in comedy 'everything happens because of the poet'.

Sentimentality

Is sentimental art therefore bad art? While 'sentimentality' originally simply meant 'full of feeling', it has acquired a negative connotation, and that makes it a challenging topic within aesthetics. Oscar Wilde, for example, describes a sentimental person as someone 'who desires to have the luxury of an emotion without paying for it'. It is exactly this that critics seem to worry about most, that 'sentimentality' involves some kind of dishonesty. Are we misrepresenting the world when we look at it sentimentally? Are we being overly emotional where it is inappropriate? Popular sentimental objects include children and animals. But aren't they really cute?

History
of Ideas

Buddhism

A man wishes to cross a wide expanse of water. There is a near shore that looks dangerous and uninviting, but the farther shore promises to be a good and safe place. With arduous, time-consuming effort he builds a raft and paddles across to the far shore. When he gets there, he understands that the raft can now be discarded. With the parable of the raft, the Buddha explains what Buddhism is all about. It is not about the teaching or dogma, but about improving human lives. The teaching is just a means to an end: alleviating human suffering. Nonetheless, the Buddhist tradition has given us some magnificent philosophy, so enjoy the passage on the raft.

Confucianism

Who are you? What gives your life meaning? The classical Confucians knew where to look for the answers. Life is about human relationships, and you are whoever you are to the people around you: a friend, sibling, colleague, parent, citizen or romantic partner. The list is extensive. The Confucians urge us to think clearly about the commitments, the specific obligations and privileges that come with our positions in these relationships. Therefore, there is no one-size-fits-all recipe for being a good person. Think about what you owe to those around you, and make the most of your life with them.

Daoism (Taoism)

Laozi, the supposed author of the most famous Chinese book of all time, the *Daodejing* (*Tao-te-ching*), can be credited with having given it the least promising beginning of any book, ever. He tells us that he wants to discuss the natural course of all things, which cannot be treated like anything we know, so that description and naming will fail. In other words, I have something extremely important to talk about, but unfortunately, I won't really be able to do it. Intriguing. Frustrating. Yet honest. The classical Daoists are great critics of the optimism of other philosophical schools, showing up the limits of language, knowledge, ethics and politics.

Presocratics

Do you understand how a car works? Perhaps you've had to jump-start the engine or change the spark plugs of a car. It is relatively easy to figure out what such individual elements do. However, to really grasp what is going on, you need to know how everything is connected and what the individual parts do in the grand scheme of the whole. A simple drawing of an internal combustion engine would do the trick. This is the kind of thing in which the earliest Western philosophers, who formed vibrant communities in Turkey and Greece, were interested. Not for cars, of course, but for the world: what is the principle that underlies all things?

Socratic Method

Socrates was a midwife: 'Have you never heard that I am the son of a midwife ... and that I practise the same trade? ... My concern is not with the body but with the soul that is experiencing birth pangs.' In talking to many of his fellow citizens, Socrates realized that, without good reason, everybody believed their opinion to be the truth. Pretending to be ignorant, he simply kept questioning every step of their argument. Soon his interlocutors became entangled in their own bad reasoning but were able to replace it gradually with better arguments, giving birth to really good ideas. Insistent, non-aggressive questioning is the key. Try it – it works a treat.

Platonism

It is fair to say that without Plato and Aristotle we wouldn't be thinking the way we do. However, at the centre of Plato's thought is an idea that is difficult to understand. He believed that there are two realms of existence, and that all things we perceive in the world of sense experience are imperfect copies of blueprints that exist in an external realm of ideas. For example, there is no perfect justice in the world, but we recognize instances of justice because we can relate them to an idea of perfect justice. The task of philosophers is to understand and communicate these perfect ideas.

Aristotelianism

Aristotle is something of a philosophical superhero. He gave systematic structure to all areas of philosophy, from metaphysics to epistemology and political theory. He invented formal logic, and did it so well that for more than 1,500 years nobody made any substantial improvements to it. He laid the groundwork for biology, physics and psychology. His complex theories of drama and of ethics are as relevant and as hotly debated as ever. And yet, from the twelfth to the seventeenth centuries his work was so revered that it held back Copernican theory and the development of modern science. Any great thought that turns into dogma has the potential to do more harm than good.

Stoicism

No other early school of philosophy has had advocates as socially diverse as Stoicism. Two of the most memorable include a slave, Epictetus, and the Roman emperor Marcus Aurelius. Stoics tell us in no uncertain terms that we must be indifferent to events that affect us but over which we have no control, whether it be a beating or a lottery win. We should focus only on what is within our power to change, since that is where our responsibility lies. Stoics champion three core values that all should adopt: *ataraxia*, peace of mind; *autarkia*, self-sufficiency; and *apatheia*, freedom from external conditions.

Scholasticism

If you want to have a good discussion, you need more than good rhetorical skills; you must also be able to listen. The Scholastics never let anyone get away with not listening. They had a strict method for philosophical discourse. A motion was put forward, such as 'The earth is flat'. Then arguments on both the affirmative and the negative side were examined. However, each new speaker had to summarize the previous speaker's arguments before they could put forward their own. In this way, everybody could be satisfied that their opponent had listened to their reasons, could reconstruct them fairly and would not be able to ignore them, but would be forced to respond to them. And that's a good conversation.

Enlightenment

'*Sapere aude!*' – 'Dare to use your own reason!' – was the battle cry of the Enlightenment. Immanuel Kant was a builder and a critic of the Enlightenment. Despite the age's great achievements, he understood that it was no time for complacency. Instead of making full use of the rational faculties that we all have, he bemoans the fact that we continue to live in 'self-incurred tutelage', which he defines as the 'inability to make use of [our] understanding without direction from another', instead of learning to think for ourselves. That was the eighteenth century; how are we doing now?

Positivism

The Positivist philosopher Auguste Comte had strong views on where humanity is going. His law of three stages outlines the development we undergo in our quest for truth. He believes that we progress as we pass through three historical phases, each with its own way of explaining the world. From the theological stage, when we make sense of the world by recourse to religious assumptions, we move on to the metaphysical stage, when philosophy predominates. Finally, we arrive at the positive stage, when we practise 'science grounded in observation'.

Marxism

'The mode of production of material life conditions the general process of social, political and intellectual life. It is not the consciousness of men that determines their existence, but their social existence that determines their consciousness.' At the heart of Marx's thought is the theory of 'historical materialism'. History is a sequence of stages that build on one another. We move through these stages driven forward not by ideas but by economic conditions, the material circumstances of our lives. They frame the way we think about the world and ourselves, and motivate us to act.

Pragmatism

If by now you are under the impression that philosophy has very little practical use, think again. The Pragmatists' main concern is thinking about real-life practical differences that the truth or falsehood of a theory would make in the world. So theory becomes subordinated to practice. The results of our actions in the world will reveal to us the truth and meaning of opinions, concepts and statements. We cannot understand anything unless we consider it in the context of concrete actions and their effects.

Analytical Philosophy

All philosophers analyse. The label 'analytical philosophy', however, is an umbrella term for a diverse tradition of thinkers who roughly take the following approach in trying to understand the underlying nature of reality. The way we perceive the world depends on our mental furniture. Analytical philosophers say that therefore, to understand reality, we must understand the nature of thought, and to understand the nature of thought we must analyse the way it is expressed in language.

Phenomenology

'To the things themselves!' Edmund Husserl's slogan points us in the right direction. Husserl thought that reality could be understood by examining the structures of consciousness. Phenomenologists try to explain why things appear to us the way they do. They analyse which parts of these phenomena are subjective and which are essential 'things themselves'. For example, when I think of a house, I may automatically picture my grandmother's house and recall all the lovely associations – ticking grandfather clocks and the aroma of warm cookies – that come with it. Phenomenologists will analyse which elements of this conscious experience are personal to me. What remains must be 'house'. This method has proved useful for understanding first-person experience in many contexts, among them the workplace, illness, disability and stress.

Existentialism

'As Gregor Samsa awoke one morning from uneasy dreams he found himself transformed in his bed into a gigantic insect.' Franz Kafka's *Metamorphosis* is a great allegory for Existentialism. Martin Heidegger reminds us that we are 'cast into' the world; much in our lives is random and unexpected, and we're not in control. When Jean-Paul Sartre says that 'existence precedes essence', he means that human beings must 'make' themselves. There is no essence that determines what or who we are. We freely choose what to do under the conditions that prevail, and we will become what we have done.

Postmodernism

In 1979, Jean-François Lyotard introduced the term 'postmodernism' into philosophical discourse. It is an -ism that is hard to define – even more so than most. What makes it interesting is that it marks a departure from many of the assumptions of the Western philosophical tradition. Above all, there is a rebellion against 'grand narratives', meaning any large-scale system of thought, such as rationalism, humanism or Christianity, Marxism or capitalism. Postmodernists trust neither the intellectual promises these systems make nor the standards they set, such as ideas of unity, science, truth and meaning. So, what is left? Well may you ask.

Deconstructionism

Jacques Derrida's deconstruction is an analytical method that helps us to unmask and rethink habits of thought and cultural bias. Ideas often come in pairs of binary oppositions, such as female and male, writing and speaking, particular and universal. Traditionally, we prioritize one term over the other and thereby define one in terms of the other, for example male over female. Derrida asks us to reverse this order of priority and show how the other term is dependent on the first, such as how the idea of 'male' depends on 'female'. We thereby re-evaluate fundamental concepts that underlie all our thinking, and arrive at a new definition of them.

LAURENCE KING

Published by Laurence King Publishing
361–373 City Road
London EC1V 1LR
United Kingdom
Tel: +44 20 7841 6900
Email: enquiries@laurenceking.com
www.laurenceking.com

A catalogue record for this book is available
from the British Library.

ISBN: 978-1-78627-694-0

Design: Alex Wright

Printed in China

Laurence King Publishing is committed to
ethical and sustainable production. We are
proud participants in the Book Chain Project®.
bookchainproject.com

**BOOK
CHAIN
PROJECT**